HARMONICA

FOR

BEGINNERS

A Beginners Guide To Playing The Harmonica,

Reading Music, Scales And Playing

Various Chords Like A Pro

Tom Wheeler

Copyright © June 2020 by Tom Wheeler

All Rights Reserved.

Kindly note that the contents of this book should not be reproduced in any way or by any means without obtaining written consent from the author or his representative.

Published By:

Blue House Media

Dedication

This book is dedicated to my family and loyal readers

Table Of Contents

How To Use This Book _____ 9

Introduction _____ 11

Lesson I: Introduction To The Harmonica _____ 13

    Choosing The Right Harmonica For Purchase __ 14

    The Diatonic Harmonica _____ 14

    Chromatic Harmonica _____ 17

    Tremolo Harmonicas _____ 19

    Highly Specialized Harmonicas _____ 20

    Parts Of The Harmonica _____ 22

    The Harmonica Notations _____ 28

    The Harmonica Missing Notes _____ 31

    Remembering The Harmonica Notes _____ 33

    Holding The Harmonica Right Handed And Left Handed _____ 35

    Holding The Harmonica Left Handed _____ 35

The Covering Position _____ 36

Lesson 2: Harmonica Playing In 1st Position _____ *38*

Introduction To Harmonica Positions _____ 38

The Importance Of Harmonica Positions _____ 40

How To Work Out Harmonica Positions _____ 44

Harmonica Positions For All Keys _____ 46

Lesson 3: How To Play Single Notes On The
Harmonica_____ 47

Playing The Harmonica On A Single Note _____ 49

Sketching The Harmonica_____ 50

Harmonica Scales _____ 53

Reading Harmonica Tabs _____ 56

Popular Songs To Play On The Harmonica _____ 57

Song 1: "Mary Had A Little Lamb"_____ 57

Song 2: "Michael Row The Boat Ashore" _____ 58

Song 3: "London Bridge" _____ 59

Song 4: "Wildwood Flower"_____ 59

Song 5: "House Of The Rising Sun" _____ 60

Song 6: "Streets Of Laredo" _____ 62

Song 7: "Red River Valley" _____ 63

Song 8: "The Marines Hymn" _____ 63

Lesson 4: The Double Stops _____ *65*

Song 9: "Goodnight Ladies" _____ 65

Song 10: "Minuet" _____ 66

Lesson 5: The Vibrato _____ *67*

The Diaphragm Vibrato _____ 67

The Hand Vibrato _____ 68

The Throat Vibrato _____ 68

Song 11: "Down In The Valley." _____ 69

Song 12: "Silent Night." _____ 70

Song 13: "Jingle bells." _____ 71

Song 14: "Careless Love" _____ 72

Lesson 6: Playing The Harmonica In 2nd Position _ *73*

Oh When The Saints (In 2nd position) _____ 73

2nd Position Or Cross Harp Scale _____ 74

Song 15: "Tom Dooley" (In 2nd position)_____ 74

Lesson 7: How To Bend A Note On The Harmonica 77

Note Bending Exercise _____ 77

Note Bending On The Harmonica_____ 86

Note Bending With A Free Tongue _____ 86

Bending With A Tongue Block On The Harmonica
_____ 89

Lesson 8: Blues Harmonica _____ *93*

The Best Harmonica For Playing Blues_____ 93

Blues Harmonica Licks And Riffs _____ 96

Five Riffs Familiar To Most Blues Musician _____ 98

How To Play 12-Bar Blues On The Harmonica _101

Conclusion _____ *105*

5 Popular Songs To Play On The Harmonica____106

Song 16: "Amazing Grace" _____106

Song 17: "He's Got The Whole World" _____107

Song 18: "Roll In My Sweet Baby's Arm" _____ 108

Song 19: "I Should Have Known Better" _____ 109

Song 20: "When The Levee Breaks" _____ 111

About The Author _____ *114*

NOTES _____ *116*

How To Use This Book

To use this book, you have to follow these instructions;

Step 1

- Practice the exercises and songs in this book continually, until you are satisfied with them

Step 2

- Don't read the book hastily, follow the process gradually

Step 3

- Follow the steps listed in this book accordingly

This book will work you through how to play the harmonica, pause, and practice every chapter until you become fully established with it. It'll likely take a couple of months for the average beginner to work through the book, so don't be hasty. Spend the effort to understand the materials properly.

Introduction

Are you searching for books on how to play the harmonica? This book is the perfect introduction to the harmonica, and suitable for all beginners to get started with their first instrument!

Without any musical skills required, this easy yet comprehensive handbook is ideal for both adults and children alike!

It contains;

- Simple to follow instructions and drawings
- How to interpret and understand musical notes and signs

- Easy exercises to be followed and practised
- Reading at your own pace
- Lots of playing tips and strategies
- Easy and convenient songs to play

Follow the instructions and lessons in this book, and you will be playing the harmonica like a pro in no time.

Lesson 1: Introduction To The Harmonica

Harmonica is a characteristic of jazz. This small wind instrument is an ancestor of the acoustic guitar and has become a favorite among con artists, globetrotters, and street performers. It emerged in the United States at the same time as the birth of jazz, and its development, as well as evolution, is credited to the creative style and techniques of the jazz musicians. Today, the primary producers of diatonic harmonicas are CA Seydel Söhne, Hohner and Lee Oskar. More affordable alternatives, such as Harley Benton, are also available.

Choosing The Right Harmonica For Purchase

Although there are a lot of highly specialized harmonicas, the three most widely known types fall into one of three classifications depending on how they are tuned: diatonic, chromatic, and tremolo. We will concentrate on these while touching on some of the less common types of harmonicas.

The Diatonic Harmonica

The most popular type of harmonica you will encounter in pop, jazz, and classical music is the diatonic harmonica. Diatonic harmonicas are designed to perform with a particular key. With all that stated, overblowing and stretching methods, including playing in intermediate "stances," make it easier to play diatonic in keys as well as ways other than its "actual" key. A few players, Howard Levy and Carlos Del Junco, have developed an over-blowing technique in which to play chromatically using a modest 10-hole diatonic harmonica.

Blues harmonica players generally operate in the so-called "cross harp" or "2nd position." This means playing the harmonica, which is keyed to an ideal fourth underneath the key in which the song is written. If the song is in key C, the F harmonica will be used. Many blues have used the notations of a pentatonic scale, and playing a G-tuned harmonica leaves you open to notations that match the pentatonic C scale, particularly the notes on which you inhale to produce those shrieking "bent" notes are the key elements of the blues harmonica method.

There are quite a lot of other positions that qualified harp players are using to match up with different instruments and produce a range of effects. Cutting your hands across the harp and using your tongue to lock and unlock holes are some of the ways of creating rhythmic and harmonic effects and tones.

Many harmonica players end up with just a set of diatonic harmonicas from different brands in a variety of keys. As their price is far more moderate than say guitars, it is simple to create a set of harps to fit various types of music and situations. I recommend that you try a range of different models to see which instruments match your style of play and the sound you desire.

Chromatic Harmonica

Many chromatic harmonicas have a button-activated lever that guides air to two different gill plates, which include all of the notations in the 12-tone European scale. With considerable skill, you can play almost any scale or method using chromatic gearshift.

The bigger wood in the chromatic is quite difficult to bend and over-blow than the diatonic peers. But thanks to the lightness, the chromatic can produce some vibrant chords and effects—many blues harmonica musicians, e.g., Little Walter, Rod Piazza, and George Harmonic. Smith utilized chromatics to produce flat tones that contributed to the blues fan phrase Mississippi sax.

In possession of a jazz musician such as Toots Thielman, a chromatic harmonica is used to perform complicated jazz scales with lightning-fast rhythmic strokes that you will most likely compare with a saxophone. Stevie Wonder is also another genius of the chromatic harmonica. His harp harmonies on "Isn't She Lovely" offer a quick lesson in overwhelming techniques.

Chromatic harmonicas are far harder to play than diatonic. Thus, I suggest starting with a diatonic and stepping up once you can use a more challenging instrument. Playing first in all positions on a diatonic will make it a lot easier for you to succeed in chromatics. Although chromatics are tuned marginally to both the C and G chord, if you know all the correct scales and positions, you can play practically any song that uses the regular 12-tone scale.

Tremolo Harmonicas

Tremolo harmonicas, sometimes known as "echo" harmonicas, generate their unique shimmering sound by using two reeds for each note, one slightly sharp, and the other somewhat flat. The distinction between the waveforms produced by the combined reeds triggers a beating effect, which is quite similar to the warbling sound of a 12-string sax that has combined strings and keyed a chord apart.

Chromatic tremolo harmonicas are common to Asian popular music. Diatonic tremolo harps are often used in folk and rock music, producing a rustic tone that is perfect for playing cowboy music like "Red River Valley."

Highly Specialized Harmonicas

Although much less popular than the varieties we have mentioned. Highly specialized harmonicas are standard for use in harmonica ensembles and melodic settings. Here's a summary:

Triad Harmonicas

These are generally astronomical instruments that can create up to 48 different chords and are usually arranged in frames of four-note nodes. Typically, each note has two reeds that are tuned a chord apart. Triad harmonicas offer excellent melodic support for harmonicas orchestra.

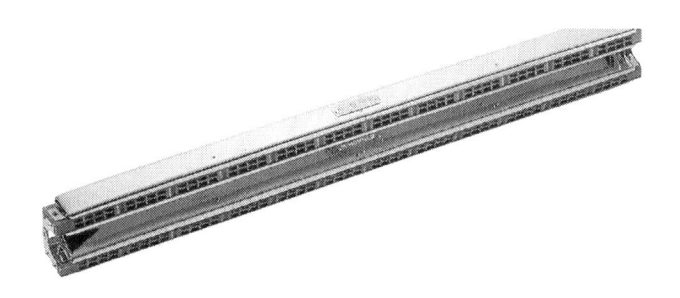

Symphonic Harmonicas

Also made to play in harmonica orchestra, these come in various pitch ranges and note-layout procedures. You're going to have to find both diatonic and chromatic brands.

Parts Of The Harmonica

The harmonica is an assembly of several pieces. Harmonica components need to be appropriately mounted to make the instrument 'airtight' and usable. The main parts of the harmonica are modified here and discussed in detail as follows: Comb, Cover

Plates, Mouthpiece, Reed Plates, Rivetting, Slider Mechanism, Valves / Wind-savers, etc.

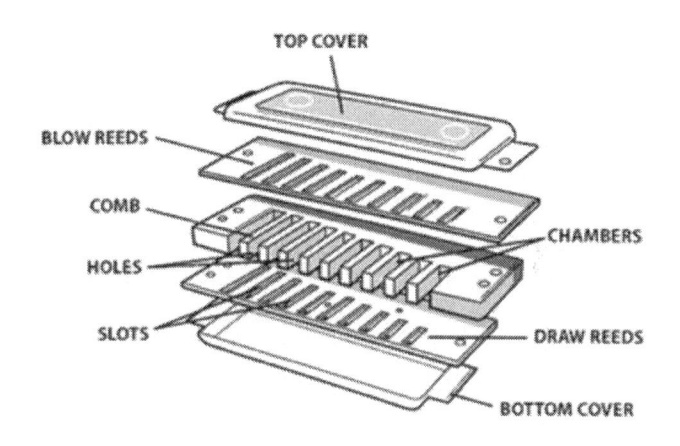

The Comb

The harmonica is designed and built towards what is known as a COMB. The comb is a vital part of the harmonica. It can be made from wood, steel, or even a type of plastic. The comb is the bit that has the openings in which you blow deeply!

Wood combs (sometimes Pear-wood) may be affected by heat. Most present harmonicas have embodied wood combs that have not been affected by heat. Steel combs are by far the most airtight combs. Wood combs are giving a softer sound to a harmonica.

The Cover Plates

These are the exterior areas of a harmonica. When you separate the cover plates, you can see the reed plates and the reeds. Cover plates secure the reeds and enable tone and air to pass through them. Cover plates can also be made of brushed stainless steel or metal that is chrome or copper-plated or blackened. There are several patterns on cover plates, some of which are considered to have excellent airflow profiles and "ergonomics" for the harmonica sound.

The Mouth-piece

The mouth-piece is the harmonica's front, its the small piece with the holes in it! The mouth-piece is used in chromatic harmonicas, and behind the mouth-piece is the slider mechanism: they are connected to the harmonica. The mouth-piece can also be placed in chrome or gold.

The Reeds

The Reeds make the harmonica note and sound. Bronze or stainless steel is used to produce reeds. Brass is the most popular material for reed production. On higher-price instruments, stainless steel reeds can be found. Brass is a smooth, sweet-tone material. Bronze reeds make the harmonic progressions of brass reeds higher than those of brass. Stainless steel is fiercer than brass and bronze and has a longer duration. At production time, the reeds are 'tuned' and can be tuned in certain situations.

The Reed Plates

Reed plates are typically made of a brass plate that is welded or grounded very plane and square. They have a few slots drilled from them to store the external reeds. Every single reed has its own slot. The reeds are gripped on the reed plate. The reed plates are either screwed or pinned to the comb. The perfect and perhaps most airtight harmonicas come with "screw-on-reed-plates."

The Slider System Button

The slider system button is a part that's activated by pushing the button at the end of the chromatic harmonicas.

The pointed and plain notes are reached by clicking the slider button. Once the slider is completely pushed in, it redirects airflow to the second set of reeds that are matched to the sharps, flats of the scale and pitch that the harmonica is matched to. As a result, once the button is pressed in, each note for each gap of the harmonica is lifted by one octave.

The Wind-savers Or Valves

The wind-savers or valves preserve the air-tightness of the instrument.

The Wood Body

The wood comb (sometimes known as pear-wood) this is the major part of the harmonica upon which the harmonica is constructed around, and the reed plates are added to it. The body or comb as it is termed can be made from plastic, steel, and wood.

The Harmonica Notations

Most new players seem to be clueless about the harmonica notations, especially since many of them tend to be "misled."

Harmonicas come with a variation of keys. The far more common harmonica key is C, its notes on the C-harmonica can be seen below. Blow signifies a note when breathing in. This note set is termed "Richter Tuning," and is often utilized for most of the harmonicas.

Hole	1	2	3	4	5	6	7	8	9	10
Blow	C	E	G	C	E	G	C	E	G	C
Draw	D	G	B	D	F	A	B	D	F	A

Take a look at holes 4 to 7. The notes from all these holes are C, D, E, F, G, A, B, C, which end up making the major scale of C. Not strange for a key C harmonica.

However, holes 1 to 4 seem to be different, beginning with hole 1, the notes are C, D, E, G, G, B, D, C. Quite challenging. Unlike holes 4 to 7, these low notes do not represent a major scale. Nevertheless, look at blow notes 1 to 4, which are C, E, G, and C. These notes create the C major chord. Blow the very first four holes to have this chord. Can you hear how all these notes seemed to agree with one another when they are played around each other?

Now take a good look at holes 4 to 7. The blow notes are C, E, G, and C. Another C chord. Likewise, the blow notes for holes 7 to 10 are also C, E, G, and C. So, all of the blow notes on the C-harmonic started from the C-chord, this is no incident, and this is why the harmonica blow notes were organized this way.

Additionally, the draw notes for holes 1 to 4 are D, G, B, and D. These notes all start from the G chord, which is crucial if playing the C key. Blow and draw on holes 1 to 4 continuously. Can you notice how well these two chords seem to match each other?

Having provided these chords in the bottom four holes while allowing a full scale in the centre holes. This is the essential motive behind the Richter tuning setup used for most harmonicas.

The Harmonica Missing Notes

As stated earlier, the alignment of the harmonica to provide chords implies that specific notes are "missing," especially in the lower holes. Nevertheless, a popular harmonica method called "bending" enables these missing notes to be played.

Bending the harmonica notes requires changing the position of the tongue, the shape of the lips, and the stress of the breath, which is quite tricky for harmonica students.

The bending of a note reduces its pitch. Bending is often taken on draw holes 1, 2, 3, 4, and 6 and blow holes 8, 9, and 10. The pattern below reveals the notes popularly acquired by bending the C-harmonica.

Hole	1	2	3	4	5	6	7	8	9	10
Blow	C	E	G	C	E	G	C	E	G	C
Blow bend								Eb	F#	Bb
Draw	D	G	B	D	F	A	B	D	F	A
Draw	Db	F#	Bb	Db		Ab				
Draw		F	A							
Draw			Ab							

The frequent blow and draw notes for the C-harmonica can be seen in bold. Having a look at the draw bends, note that one additional note is applicable from holes 1, 4, and 6. Most players still bend hole five a little, yet practically speaking, an additional note is not applicable by doing this.

The double hole draw enables two additional curved notes, whereas the 3-hole draw allows three additional bent notes. Managing these notes requires practice, but the skill is understood with most experienced players.

The single additional bent note is applicable in blowholes 8, 9, and 10. A deficient number of players can also get two separate bent notes from the 10th blow.

More notes were applicable using an effective method termed over-blowing.

Remembering The Harmonica Notes

Since there are 12 harmonica keys available, each of which has different notes, the challenge of trying to remember them all would seem daunting to new players. Well, great news. It is not necessary to recall all of the notes. Most players would have been hard-pressed to name them, particularly to the less commonly used keys.

Most players instead recall "scale degrees." These are firmly identified with the "do re mi fa so la ti do," which several people study at school. This method permits tunes and solos to be comprehended without requiring the note names for explicit music keys.

All that is required is affection for the instrument, diligence, proper guidance, and similar melodic companions. All these can be found.

Holding The Harmonica Right Handed And Left Handed

Setting The Numbers On The Harmonica

Take your ten holes diatonic and ensure that the numbers at the top are facing you from 1 – 10. The harmonica moves from small notes at hole 1 to high notes at hole 10.

Holding The Harmonica Left Handed

Keep the harmonica between your index finger and your thumb. Keep your index finger and thumb near to the back of the harmonica as necessary. This is going to create a space for your mouth at the front.

- Place your middle finger behind the harmonica. Keep your middle finger at

the back of the harmonica while touching your thumb to prevent the harmonica from sliding back.
- Curve your fingers behind the harmonica
- Cure your fingers round to structure a loose cup shape behind the harmonica.
- Place your right thumb on the right side of the harmonica
- Keep the right thumb on the right side of the harmonica in the pinkie toe-up position.

The Covering Position

Curve your right hand over the harmonica, covering the top three holes. Cover the thumb hole with your right hand while doing this.

When you do this correctly, you will have a silent sound if your hands are closed. If not, the air is sneaking out somewhere. Check-in a mirror while playing and see if you can see any sneaky air gaps that could slip through.

With that stated, let's move to the next lesson.

Lesson 2: Harmonica Playing In 1st Position

Harmonica positions are indeed a significant component of harmonica music history since they represent a primarily overlooked concept.

Introduction To Harmonica Positions

Harmonica positions are practically how well the harmonica players can play on just a specific harmonica with different scales. To explain: The tuning is built to enable as more flexibility is necessary when playing a C harmonica, including several different chords and scales.

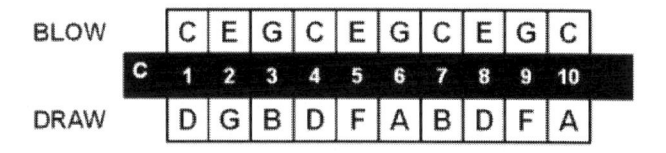

BLOW	C	E	G	C	E	G	C	E	G	C
C	1	2	3	4	5	6	7	8	9	10
DRAW	D	G	B	D	F	A	B	D	F	A

The lowest note is a C, and the highest note is also a C. That very harmonica would be described as tuned in C-major according to the actual Richter tuning. As a result, the C major scale is quite simple to follow from holes 1 to 10 all the way; we may define the C note as the natural tonic.

But what if we were planning to play a song in another key (in G, for example)? Well, we ought to make sure we begin and end all the scales we have played on G note (two draws, three blows, six blows, and nine blows) and play several G chords as well. The G note will become a significant part of our music. We will have to use a completely different set of holes to play the G major scale on a C harmonica similar to the holes we would use to play the C major scale. That is, we need to change places.

Thus, a position (in harmonica theory) seems to be just a specific way to play music in a different key compared to the harmonica key you use. Playing songs on a C harmonica key is known as 1st position (also known as a straight guitar). The 2nd position (also known as Cross Harp) is used to play music in the key of G on a C harmonica.

The Importance Of Harmonica Positions

It is vital to show a primary difference between playing the harmonica and playing an instrument like a piano. When playing the piano, we often use different keys to play multiple scales. Nevertheless, when pressing a key on a keyboard, you already know what sound will be made since each key is only tuned to play one particular note.

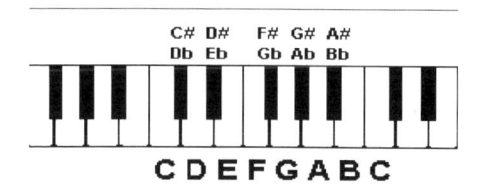

```
        C# D#   F# G# A#
        Db Eb   Gb Ab Bb
  C D E F G A B C
```

This applies to harmonicas to some extent. When you blow on hole four on a C harmonica, you know you're going to play a C. When you draw on hole two on a C harmonica, you know that you're going to play a G, and so on. All these changes, once you choose not to include a C harmonica. What if you use an F harmonica?

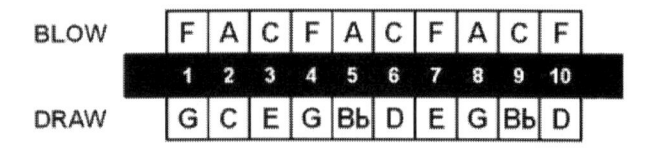

BLOW	F	A	C	F	A	C	F	A	C	F
	1	2	3	4	5	6	7	8	9	10
DRAW	G	C	E	G	Bb	D	E	G	Bb	D

All notes on an F harmonica are different. When you look closely, you will find out that you need to play in 2nd position to play any C scales, and this is because the holes that play G on the C harmonica (two draws, three blasts, six blasts, and nine blows) now play C on the F harmonica.

This is the primary difference concerning playing songs on the harmonica. Also, you will have to play in different positions based on the key of the harmonica itself, and since there are 12 different keys (A, Bb, B, C, Db, etc.), there are 12 different positions on the harmonica.

When all the harmonicas are tuned like that of a C-harmonica, there is really no difference between scale and position. However, there are, in reality, 12 different tunings (one in every key), which signifies the only thing that is left constant between the different tunings is the sequence of the holes that you use to play a specific position.

For instance, to play 1st Position (Straight Harp) on the F-harmonica, you will use precisely the very same holes just like you would use to play 1st position on the C-harmonica. Nevertheless, you might have produced two different scales (F and C, respectively). To play 2nd Position (Cross Harp) on the F-harmonica, you will use precisely the very same holes as you might use to play 2nd position on the C-harmonica. Nevertheless (again), you would have produced two different scales (C and G, respectively).

How To Work Out Harmonica Positions

You are probable to ever use beyond the first five positions; in fact, many harmonica players rarely use anything besides 1st, 2nd, and 4th positions. That stated it's still good to learn how everything comes together.

In the previous section, showing various harmonica scales, just the first five positions are covered although, they are extensive and include the main, minor, blues, and pentatonic scales. The last one is quite common in country music.

To measure the key of a specific position, you simply count the ideal 5th (7 semitones) from the tonic of the initial position. For instance, the 1st position on the C-harmonica is in key C, so to figure out the 2nd position key we will just count seven semitones from C this brings us to G. To also determine the 3rd position key on the C-harmonica, we're just counting another seven semitones from G this brings us to D.

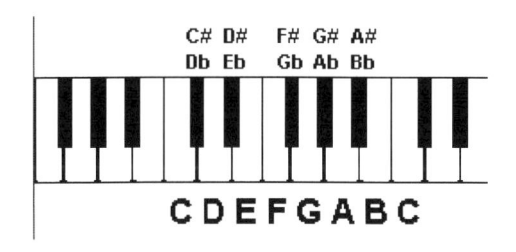

C# D# F# G# A#
Db Eb Gb Ab Bb

C D E F G A B C

You can also apply this logic, which is likely what you're going to do in practice. For instance, if you will like to play 2nd Position

Blues in an A key, you'll only count seven semitones out of A; this will bring you down to D. So, to play the 2nd position in A key, then you need to use D-harmonica.

Now you know so much about harmonica positions than about 95 percent of all harmonica players (and few other professionals). Pat yourself on the back, because you've come a very long way.

Harmonica Positions For All Keys

Key of Song (Band)	1st Position	2nd Position	3rd Position	4th Position	5th Position	12th Position
Ab	Ab	Db	F#	B	E	Eb
A	A	D	G	C	F	E
Bb	Bb	Eb	Ab	Db	F#	F
B	B	E	A	D	G	F#
C	C	F	Bb	Eb	Ab	G
Db	Db	F#	B	E	A	Ab
D	D	G	C	F	Bb	A
Eb	Eb	Ab	Db	F#	B	Bb
E	E	A	D	G	C	B
F	F	Bb	Eb	Ab	Db	C
F#	F#	B	E	A	D	Db
G	G	C	F	Bb	Eb	D

Lesson 3: How To Play Single Notes On The Harmonica

Once you begin playing the harmonica, you'll notice it's simple to play 2 or 3 holes at the very same time. However, hitting a single, smooth note can be very challenging; this is because the holes in the harmonica are tiny and tight!

There are two main ways to play single notes:

- Mouth Blocking
- Tongue Blocking

The Strong Relaxed Mouth-Piece

The position of the mouth that we will use to play single notes is the "The Strong Relaxed

Mouth-Piece" Below is a brief overview of this method:

Position the harmonica deep into your mouth.

Place the harmonica 30 degrees back to the lower lip such that the lower lip "unfolds."

Hold the upper lip comfortable and deep.

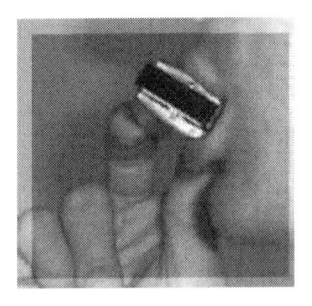

It is very vital to keep the upper lip comfortable. The experience of educating dozens of harmonica students has taught me that all those who tighten their lips will needlessly face challenges, we only use the lower lip to obstruct the unwanted holes, and the upper lip stays Completely Relaxed.

Playing The Harmonica On A Single Note

- Place the harmonica in your mouth, with a strong, relaxed mouth-piece.
- Place your lower lip slightly by bringing the edges of your lip nearer together. The concept is that your lower lip will block holes 3 and 5 when playing hole 4. The upper lip should be relaxed.
- Pull the harmonica out of your mouth and look in a mirror.
- Adjust the position of your tongue to see if it helps you out.

- Try opening wide your mouth by saying ahhh or ohhh.

Sketching The Harmonica

Step 1: Sketch Out A Rectangle, More Like A Prism

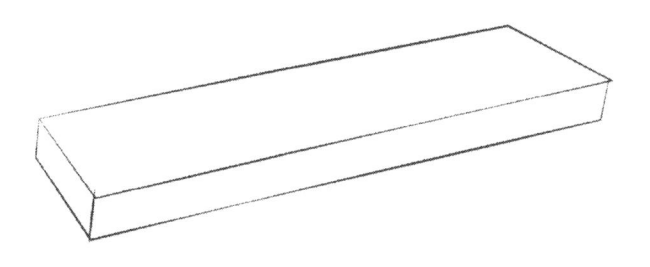

Step 2: Draw The Very Same Pattern As The One Above, But Reduced In Size.

Step 3: Improve The Shape Sketched In Step 1

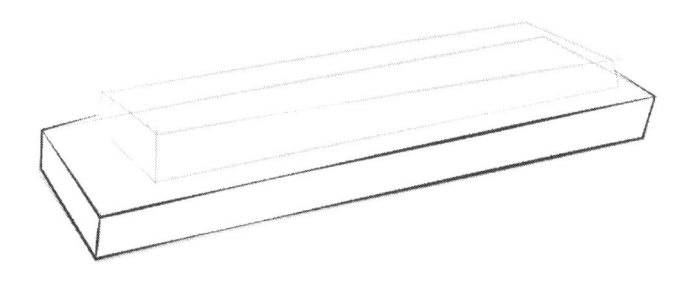

Step 4: Improve The Shape Sketched In Step 2

Step 5: Sketch 4 Narrow Lines On One Part Of The Rectangle

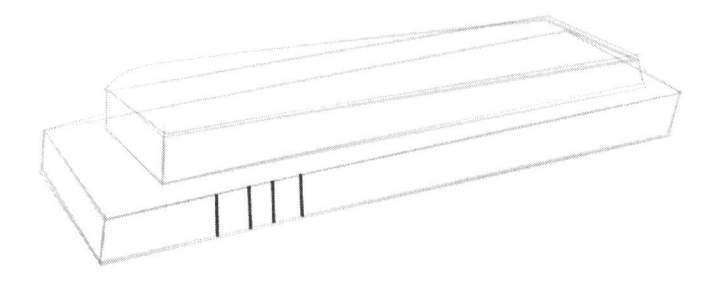

Step 6: Repeat The Same Step In Step 5

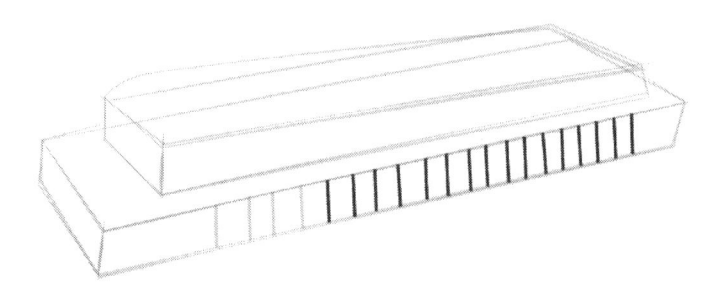

Step 7: Improve The Drawing As Shown In The Picture Above

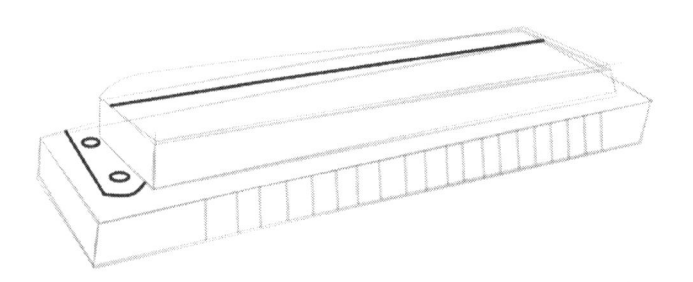

Step 8: Make The Appropriate Changes And Conclude The Drawing

Harmonica Scales

Throughout this lesson, I'm going to assist you in understanding the scale so that you can learn your favorite music more quickly.

Reasons For Learning Harmonica Scales

Most people just have an allergic response to studying some music theory whatsoever, choosing to say, "I only play what I experience, man." They seem to think that knowing how music operates can somehow ruin the joy they feel in the song. Many are very strict about the "laws" of music, all concerned with scales and theories, but they've failed to notice how to enjoy the moment.

The most satisfying sequence is in the midst of these two things. Music is, in the end, an art, not physics. Music is about sharing feelings and being linked to people. The best way to approach music would be to have fun in the process.

Playing the harmonica is quite different from playing the guitar or a keyboard since we can't see what we do with our eyes. Studying a scale can become a useful way of helping us understand what we do when we play.

The Major Scales

One good thing about the harmonica is that, even though it's a minimal instrument, it does have a 3-octave range. This is a wider variety than the average artist! How incredible it is that we can get several notes out of a tiny and compact instrument.

This also turned out that the center octave, starting with the 4th blow, is the simplest way to play the C major scale since it doesn't involve any bends. The smaller octave, starting with the 1st blow, needs two separate draw bends (gaps 3 & 4), as well as the upper octave, which requires a blow bend (hole 7).

The center octave, nevertheless, with just a little self-control, is a straightforward scale that most beginners can try to play.

Reading Harmonica Tabs

Below you will see harmonica tabs for major scale:

4 -4 5 -5 6 -6 -7 7

Also, see that when we play the scale-up, we blow but then bring any of the first three gaps (gaps 4,5, & 6), but it shifts, and we draw, so when we blow, we get to hole 7.

Below you will see also harmonica tabs for going down the major scale

7 -7 -6 6 -5 5 -4 4

Tab	Interval

4	One
-4	Two
5	Three
-5	Four
6	Five
-6	Six
-7	Seven
7	One

With that stated, I believe you're ready for the next lesson.

Popular Songs To Play On The Harmonica

Song 1: "Mary Had A Little Lamb"

Harmonica Type: **Diatonic**

Key: **C**

5B	**4D**	**4B**	**4D**	**5B**	**5B**	**5B**
Ma -	ry	had	a	lit -	tle	lamb

4D	**4D**	**4D**	**5B**	**6B**	**6B**
Lit -	tle	lamb	lit -	tle	lamb

5B	**4D**	**4B**	**4D**	**5B**	**5B**	**5B**
Ma -	ry	had	a	lit -	tle	lamb

4D	**4D**	**5B**	**4D**	**4B**
Fleece	was	white	as	snow.

Song 2: "Michael Row The Boat Ashore"

Harmonica Type: **Diatonic**

Key: **C**

```
4 5      6   5   6    -6 6      5  6 -6 6
Michael, row the boat ashore, Hallelujah.
5 6      6   5   -5   5-4      4 -4 5-4 4
Michael, row the boat ashore, Hallelujah.

4 5      6    5   6    -6  6       5  6 -6 6
Sister, help to trim the sails, Hallelujah.
5 6      6    5   -5   5   -4      4 -4 5-4 4
Sister, help to trim the sails, Hallelujah.

River Jordan's deep and wide, Hallelujah.
Milk and honey on the other side, Hallelujah.

River Jordan's chilly and cold, Hallelujah.
Chills the body, but warms the soul, Hallelujah.

Then you'll fear the trumpet sound, Hallelujah.
Sinner row to save your soul, Hallelujah.
```

Song 3: "London Bridge"

Harmonica Type: **Diatonic**

Key: **C**

```
6   -6    6     -5  5  -5    6
London Bridge is falling down

-4  5     -5
Falling down

5   -5    6
Falling down

6   -6    6     -5  5  -5    6
London Bridge is falling down

-4  6   5   4
My fair lady.
```

Song 4: "Wildwood Flower"

Harp Type: **Diatonic**

Key: **C**

```
5    5   -5   6   -6   7  5  -5   5   -4 5    -4     4
```
Oh, I'll entwine with my mingles and waving black hair.
```
   5   -5   6 -6   7  5    -5   5   -4 5   -4    4
```
With the roses so red and the lilies so fair.

And the myrtles so bright with emerald dew
The pale and the leader and eyes look like blue.

Oh, I'll dance, I will sing and my laugh shall be gay
I will charm ev'ry heart, in his crown I will sway
```
   6  7   8      8  -8    7     6    6 -6 7   -6    6
```
When I woke from my dream and my idol was clay.
```
 5   5    5     5    5
```
All portions of love then had all flown away.

Oh, he taught me to love him and promised to love
And to cherish me over all others above
How my heart now is wond'ring misery can tell
He's left me no warning, no words of farewell.

Oh, he taught me to love him and called me his flow'r
That was blooming to cheer him through life's dreary hour
Oh, I'm longing to see him through life's dark hour
He's gone and neglected this pale wildwood flower.

Song 5: "House Of The Rising Sun"

Harmonica Type: **Diatonic**

Key: **C**

How To Play The Harmonica Like A Pro

```
  5   -6  -7   7    8   -8   -6  -6
There is  a  house  in  New Orleans,
-10  -10 -10   9    8    8
They call the Rising Sun.
-10 -10  -10  -7   7    8  -8-6 -6 -6   -6
And it's been the ruin of many a poor boy,
 -6  -6  -6  6 5  6   -6
And God, I  know  I'm one.

-10 10 -10  9  7  -8 -6
My  mother was a tailor,
 -10  -10  9    8    8
Sewed  my new blue jeans.
-10 -10 -10   9  7   -8  -6 -6  -67
My   fa-ther was a  gam--bl-in' man,
-6  -6   6 5 6  -6
Down in New Orleans.

-10 -10 -10 -10    9   7  -8  -6  -6
Now the onl--y  thing a gambler needs,
-10 -10 -10 -10   9  8   8
Is   a  suitcase and a trunk,
-10 -10 -10 -10   9    7   -8-6
And the   o-nly time he'll be,
-6  -6  7   -6  -6   -6  6 5 6   -6
Sa-tisfied, is when he's a-ll a drunk.

-5   -6 -7   7    8   -8  -6
Oh mother tell your  children,
-6  -10 -10 -10  9  8     8
Not  to do what  I have done.
  10   -7   7    8   -8  -6 -6-6-6
Spend your lives in sin and misery,
-6 -6    -6  -6  6   5  6   -6
In the house of the rising sun.
```

61

```
{Word's}   -10 -10  -10  9   7   -8  -6
Well I've  got one foot on the platform.
-10 -10   -10   9  8    8
The other foot on the train.
-10 -10 -10   9    7 -8    -6 -6  7
I'm go--in' back to New  Orleans,
 7  -6   -6  6   5  6     -6
To wear that ba-ll and chain.
-10   -10 -10 -10   9    7 -8  -6 -6
Well there is   a house in New Orleans,
 -10   -10 -10   9  8    8
They call  the Rising Sun.
-10 -10   -10 -10   9   7 -8-6 -6 -6    7
And it's been the ruin of many a poor boy,
 -6   -6 -6 6   5  6   -6
And God, I kn-ow I'm one.
```

Song 6: "Streets Of Laredo"

Harmonica Type: Diatonic

Key: **Any Key**

```
   The Streets Of Laredo

 6 6 -5   5    -5    6 -5    5     -4  4 -3  3
As I___ walked out  in the streets of La-re-do,

 3 4   4    -4   5 -5  5 -4   4   -4   6   6  -5
as I walked out in La-re-do one day, I spied a

 5   -5   6  -5    5    -4   4  -3  3    3
poor cow-boy all wrapped in white lin-en, all

   4   -3   4   -4   5  -5  5   -3 -4   4
wrapped in white lin-en as cold as the day.
```

Song 7: "Red River Valley"

Harmonica Type: **Diatonic**

Key: **G**

```
 3    4    5    5    5    5
From this val-ley they say

-4   5   -4   4
you are go-ing,

 3  4    5    4    5    6
We will miss your bright eyes

-5   5      -4
and sweet smile.

 6   -5   5   5   -4   4   -4
For they say you are tak-ing

 5   6   -5
the sun-shine

 3   3   3      -3
That has bright-ened

 4  -4   5  -4   4
our path-ways a-while.
```

Song 8: "The Marines Hymn"

Harmonica Type: **Diatonic**

Key: **C**

```
 4    5      6      6  6    6  67 6
From the Halls of Mon te zum a,
 5   -5     6      6  -5 -4 4
To the Shores of Tri po li;
45    6     6      6      67  6
We fight our coun try's bat tles
 5   -5  6     6       -5    -4  4
In the air, on land, and sea;
 7   -7    -6     -5  -6    -5  6  -6  6
First to fight for right and fre  e   dom
 7   -7    -6    -5  -6  7    6
And to  keep our hon or clean;
 4 5    6      6  6    6  67  6
We are proud to claim the ti tle
5  -5 6  6     -5    -4   4
Of U ni ted States Ma rines
```

Let's move to the next lesson.

Lesson 4: The Double Stops

A double stop is a process of playing two notes at the same time with necessarily equal power. Double stops can also be performed utilizing bent notes as well as mixtures of bent and unbent natural notes, particularly on holes 1-4.

Song 9: "Goodnight Ladies"

Harmonica Type: **Chromatic**

Key: **G**

```
 -4     3    -1  3      -4    3    -3  -3
Good night, la-dies; good night la-dies;
 -4     3    4   4
Good night la-dies,
  4    -4  -4   3     -3    -2*   3
we're go-ing to leave you now.
-4   -3  3   -3   -4  -4   -4
Mer-ri-ly we roll a-long,
 -3 -3  -3      -4  -5   -5
roll a-long, roll a-long.
-4   -3  3   -3   -4  -4   -4
Mer-ri-ly we roll a-long
-3    -3    -4    -3    3
o'er the deep blue sea.
```

Song 10: "Minuet"

Harmonica Type: **Diatonic**

Key: **A**

```
6   4   -4   5   -5   6
4   -6  -5   6   -6   -7   7   4
-5  6   -5   5   -4   5
-5  5   -4   4   -3
4   -4  5    3   -3
6   4   -4   5   -5   6
4   -6  -5   6   -6   -7   7   4
-5  6   -5   5   -4   5
-5  5   -4   4   -4
5   -4  4    -3  4
```

Lesson 5: The Vibrato

A Perfect vibrato is difficult to attain at first; however, it is crucial to put a level headed quality to your playing. There are three known types of vibrato; hand, diaphragm, and throat. The throat vibrato is by far the most commonly used and the most outstanding example.

The Diaphragm Vibrato

The diaphragm vibrato was attributed to the rapid tension and tranquillity of the diaphragm muscles. I've never known anyone to use this technique, but if I were a doubter, I would say you don't mind the vibrato diaphragm – you're not going to miss anything.

The Hand Vibrato

This entails pushing the harmonica backward and forward (towards and away from the guts) without trying to break the contact between your lips and the harp. It can be done quickly, or gradually, to add quality to a silent piece. Still, this is not a commonly used technique, and, in my personal experience, it remains on the tacky side of the street. You're not missing a lot if you don't try this technique.

The Throat Vibrato

Here's where it is. It's the basic vibrato that every player must understand. I remember when I started; the blow bends and the throat vibrato were the two biggest puzzles in the harp play. You place the barrow down and then get trapped in it. But, if I could get there, so can you.

Throat vibrato is an operated effect of staccato. It's also linked to bending (particularly on draw notes) and even to a glottal stop because a great deal of control is attained from the back of the throat.

It's going to be challenging at first. However, think of an opera singer, take a deep breath and stay strong. You can also milk it once you get it. In its intense form, it can be paired with draw bending to 'choke' the harmonica.

With that stated, let move into songs using the above vibratos

Song 11: "Down In The Valley."
Harmonica Type: **Diatonic**

Key: **Any**

```
  3   4 -4   5    4    5  -4    4 -4    3      -3
Down in the val-ley, val-
ley so low, hang your
 -4 -5 -4      -3   4    -4   4
head o-ver, hear the wind blow.
  3   4   -4   5    4    5 - 4   4   -4
Hear the wind blow, boys, hear the wind blow,
  3    -3   -4 -5 -4    -3   4   -4   4
Hang your head o-ver, hear the wind blow.
```

Song 12: "Silent Night."

Harmonica Type: **Diatonic**

Key: **C**

```
6 -6 6         5      6 -6 6        5
Si -lent night, Ho -ly night,
-8  -8  -7   7   7   6
All is calm, All is bright
 -6   -6   7 -7-6    6  -6   6   5
Round yon Vir -gin Moth -er and Child,
-6 -6  7  -7  -6  6 -6   6   5
Ho-ly in-fant so tender and mild
 -8   -8   -9     -8 -7  7   8
Sleep in heaven-en-ly peace,
7  6   5  6   -5 -4   4
Sleep in heav-en-ly peace
```

Song 13: "Jingle bells."

Harmonica Type: Any

Key: Any

```
-4 -7 -6 6 -4
dashing through the snow
-4 -4 -4 -7 -6 6 5
on a one-horse open sleigh
5 7 -7 -6 -8
over the hills we go
-8 -8 7 -6 -7
laughing all the way
-4 -7 -6 6 -4
bells on bob-tails ring
-4 -7 -6 6 5 5
making spirits bright
5 7 -7 -6 -8 -8 -8
oh what fun it is to ride
-8 8 -8 7 -6 6 -8
and sing a sleighing song tonight
-7 -7 -7 -7 -7 -7
jingle bells, jingle bells
-7 -8 6 -6 -7
jingle all the way
7 7 7 7 7 -7 -7
oh what fun it is to ride
-7 -7 -6 -6 -7 -6
on a one-horse open sleigh
-7 -7 -7 -7 -7 -7
jingle bells, jingle bells
-7 -8 6 -6 -7
jingle all the way
7 7 7 7 7 -7 -7
oh what fun it is to ride
-7 -7 -6 -6 6
on a one-horse open sleigh
```

Song 14: "Careless Love"

Harmonica Type: Diatonic

Key: C

```
5    5     4  -3    3  -3   -4   4
Oh Love, Oh Love, Oh Care-less Love,
 5   -5    6   6  -6   6    -4
Love Oh, Love Oh Care-less Love,
 5   -5  6    6 -6    -5   4
Love, Oh Love, Oh Care-less Love,
  5  -5   6    4   -3   3   -3  -4 4
Cant you see what love has done to me,
 5   -5   6    4   -3   3   -3  -4 4
Cant you see what love has done to me.

Oh I was rich but now Im poor,
I was rich but now Im poor,
I was rich but now Im poor,
Cant you see what love has done to me,
Cant you see what love has done to me.
```

Lesson 6: Playing The Harmonica In 2nd Position Or Cross Harp

Within this position, the harmonica is played a complete 5th (seven semitones) above the marked key on the harmonica. On a C-tuned harp, the 2nd position will be in G. It is the most popularly utilized position to play blues, rock, and country. This position consists of draw notes at the lower end of the harmonica (holes 1 to 5), so it is necessary to master note bending in this position.

Oh When The Saints (In 2nd position)

↓	↓	↑	↓	↓	↓	↑	↓
2	3	4	4	2	3	4	4

↓	↓	↑	↓	↓	↓	↓	↓
2	3	4	4	3	2	3	3b

You'll notice that once we move to the next line, 'Oh when the saints go marching in,' the 'in' is bending. So here you can play in both the first and second positions, you just have to fix those bends!

2nd Position Or Cross Harp Scale

Song 15: "Tom Dooley" (In 2nd position)

Harmonica Type: **Diatonic**

Key: **G**

How To Play The Harmonica Like A Pro

```
 -4    -4   -4    5    6  -7  -7
Hang down your head, Tom Doo-ley,
 -4    -4   -4    5   6  -6
Hang down your head and cry.
 -4    -4   -4    5    6  -6  -6
Hang down your head, Tom Doo-ley,
 -7  -6    6      5-4  5   6
Poor boy, you're bound to die.
```

```
-4 -4 -4  5   6   -7   -7
I met her on the moun-tain.
-7    -4 -4  5   6   -6
and there I took her life.
-6 -4 -4  5   6   -6   -6
I met her on the moun tain,
-7    -6   6  5 -4 5    6
and stabbed her with my knife.
```

```
 -4    -4   -4    5    6  -7  -7
Hang down your head, Tom Doo-ley,
 -4    -4   -4    5   6  -6
Hang down your head and cry.
 -4    -4   -4    5    6  -6  -6
Hang down your head, Tom Doo-ley,
 -7  -6    6      5-4  5   6
Poor boy, you're bound to die.
```

```
 -4    5   6   -7  -7
This time to-mor-row,
This time to-mor-row,

 -4  -4   5    6   -6
Reck-on where I'll be.
Reck-on where I'll be,
```

75

```
-6 -6   -4   -4    5    6     -6  -6
if it hadn�-a been for   Gray-son,
        in   some lone-some val-ley,

-7 -7    -6  6   5-4    5    6
I'd a---been in Ten---nes-see.
A-hangin' on a- white oak tree.

-4    -4    -4    5    6  -7  -7
Hang down your head, Tom Doo-ley,
 -4   -4    -4    5    6  -6
Hang down your head and cry.
 -4   -4    -4    5    6  -6  -6
Hang down your head, Tom Doo-ley,
 -7  -6    6      5-4  5    6
Poor boy, you're bound to die.
```

Lesson 7: How To Bend A Note On The Harmonica

Bending notes on the harmonica can be quite challenging for most beginners. Still, the fact is, it is one of the most crucial parts in learning to play the harmonica, but before we move into note-bending on the harmonica, let's practice some note bending exercise.

Note Bending Exercise

Notes bending on the harmonica occurs in the dark corners of your mouth, with the harp obscuring the view, so seeing it involves something a little less invasive than headlamps and mirrors. Even so, you could get an idea of what is going on within your mouth by performing some secure tongue checks, and then you can attempt some breathing and vocal sounds to get you ready on the bending route.

Explore The Top Of Your Mouth

Take the tip of your tongue to the back of your top front teeth. Then move it back over the top of your mouth so that you can sense the shape of the top.

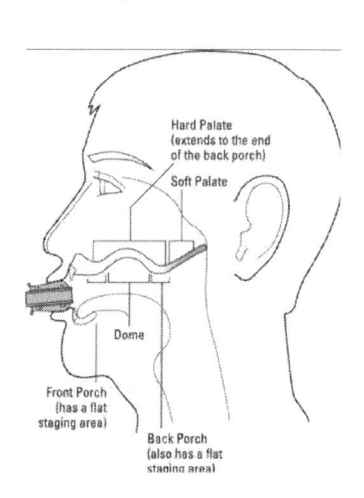

Hard Palate
(extends to the end
of the back porch)

Soft Palate

Dome

Front Porch
(has a flat
staging area)

Back Porch
(also has a flat
staging area)

Usually, if you practice note bending, you lift some part of your tongue to a position along the curves. Exceptionally low-pitched notes could bend by lifting the tongue somewhere within the backyard, whereas high notes could bend in the area of the dome or just on the front porch.

By utilizing your tongue in this manner, you can adjust your mouth to various notes by changing the size of your oral cavity, the closed area within your mouth, something like:

Tongue lifted in the mouth = wide space = low note

Tongue lifted within the mouth = narrow space = high note

Making A Decent Sounds

Simply move your tongue forward or backward, your mouth will not bend a note except you trigger the bend.

Say this: "eeee-ooh" and see what your mouth is doing.

If you utter "eee," you draw your lips far from each other to open your mouth full.

If you say the word "oh," you bring the edges of your mouth near to make a small, oval opening.

Shape your mouth to say "ooh," and then you will let the "eee" sound out. When you get the "eee" sound, you'll be directed to make some extra sounds. Here's what you're doing:

Shape your lips into a circular shape to create the "ooh" sound.

Put the tip of your tongue behind your front teeth and underneath the top of your mouth, floating underneath the front porch.

Once you have your tongue in position, try to sing a prolonged note with "eee" sound. You might have to focus on putting your tongue and holding your lips in a tiny "O" form, but it's likely going to be pretty straightforward.

Keep singing the note and drift your tongue back into your mouth, putting it up, so it sits close to the top. You can hear the "eeee" switch to "ooh" when you move your tongue backward.

Once you're at the point where you hear the "ooh" sound, hold your tongue in that position and hum "koo, koo, koo" a couple of times. Remember what is going on with your mouth. It goes up to touch the top of your mouth and temporarily obstruct the flow of air. You can notice the "k" sound as you allow the airflow by dropping your tongue gently. This "k" action is the starting point of understanding how to trigger a bend.

Use The K-Spot To Make Your Bend Activator

You're going to do all you've just done however with significant variables:

Rather than using your voice, you will whisper.

You are meant to inhale, rather than exhale.

You can notice the air flowing in your oral cavity once you slide your tongue backward as you inhale. As you slide from the "eee" sound to the "ooh" sound, you can notice the vocals change in the airflow sound, and you can also see the sound move down as you slide to "ooh"—you tune your mouth to a lower note!

Once you're at the "ooh" sound, try to sound "ookookookookoo" with one constant breath and recognize that every time you stop the flow of air, you experience a small amount of suction pulling over your throat and your top rib cage. During this level, focus on making the "coo" sound extremely slow.

As you breathe and whisper the "koo" sound, take your tongue very slowly out of the top of your mouth, such that the air can't move easily.

Your tongue will attempt to escape the gravity of the top of your mouth since the suction is pulling it back together.

Strive to maintain your tongue in that position so that you can continuously feel the flow of air as you breathe air through the reduced passing between your tongue and the top of your mouth.

With this reduced passing in the flow of air, you can unlock the bends.

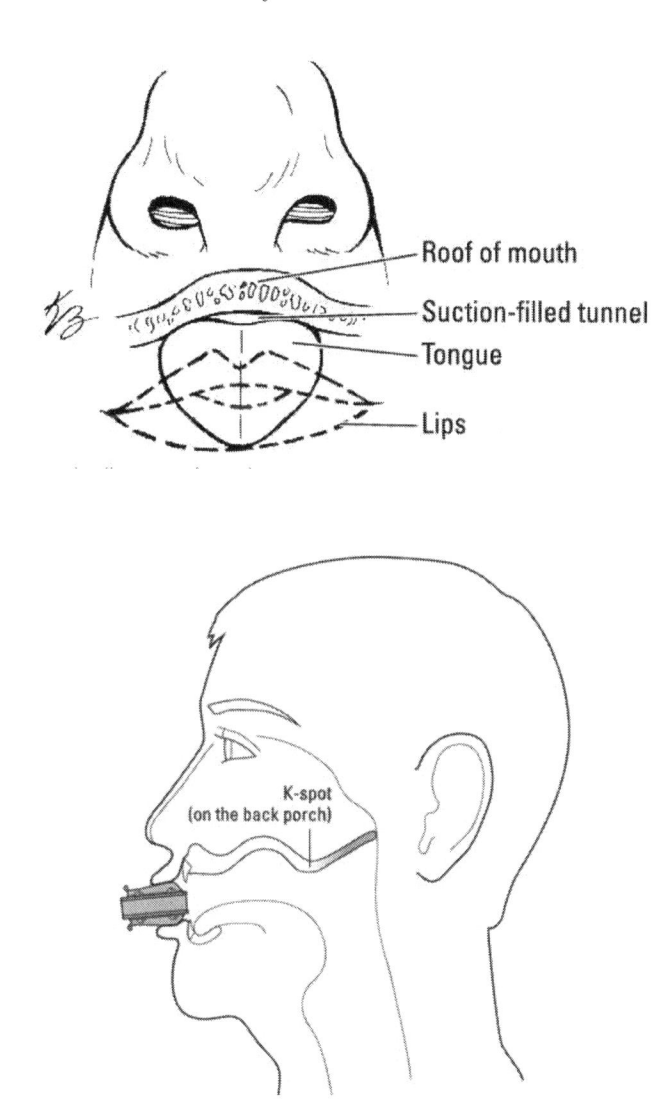

Roof of mouth
Suction-filled tunnel
Tongue
Lips

K-spot
(on the back porch)

With that stated, let move into note-bending on the harmonica

Note Bending On The Harmonica

For you to bend notes easily, you have to cover your nasal gaps and play a single note without air escaping from your lips.

Begin with Draw 4, or perhaps Draw 5 or 6, to have your very first bend. Your first inhaled bend can occur anywhere around the first six holes. However, you are most likely to be effective in the center holes since these bends within those holes are all deep bends, so you don't have to create an incredibly tiny or wide oral cavity shape for the highest and the lowest notes.

Note Bending With A Free Tongue

You should put on your most beautiful outfit and best footwear and get a fresh haircut and manicure to get set for your first bend. You can also just grab your harp, locate Hole 4, and play a long relaxing draw line, breathing softly and deeply. That would be the note you're looking to bend.

To turn that Draw 4 into a bent note, you need to do this:

- When you play Draw 4, utilize your tongue to create the "eee" sound (the note will begin to sound sharper if you put your tongue within the "eee" position).
- When you drift your tongue back to the "ooh" position, lift it marginally to generate airflow. At this level, you might hear a note slipping down in tone if the moon is in a correct phase, and your lotto numbers are accurate.

- If your tongue is in the "ooh" position, start creating the "kookookoo" sound, drag your tongue out of the top slowly, and notice the airflow pulling your tongue up. Once you feel the airflow, attempt moving the K-spot back and forth gently along the top of your mouth. You can have your first bend at a certain point along that path.

- Your first bend can happen fast, or it could end up taking days or weeks. Be patient, you're going to get it, and that will be sooner or later. In the meantime, focus on some other harmonica skills, including bending and paying attention to the sound of bent notes. When you listen, you will begin to recognize when a bent note takes place.

Bending With A Tongue Block On The Harmonica

Most harmonica players haven't learned to bend with a tongue block. They could be at the center of playing a subtle tongue-blocking effect but instead turn to a clench to play a bent note, and then go back to the tongue-blocking effect. That would be a lot of troublesome switching, and you don't need it.

Having to bend with a tongue block is never more complicated than bending with a wrinkle and it is not all that unique. What you need to do is move it to the tip of your tongue in your mouth.

Try this without the harmonica!

- Put the edge of your tongue across your lips, and your top and bottom lips should be gently closed against the upper and lower surfaces of your tongue, as well as the left side of your tongue, closed against the left corner of your mouth.
- Create an opening in the right corner of your mouth that will enable you to breathe properly.
- When you breathe in, whisper "kuh-kuh-kuh" the area at which your tongue contacts the top of your mouth is where you generate a K-spot.
- Try to create a K-spot as you breathe in. You do so by lifting the section of your tongue that says "k" next to the top of

your mouth to make you feel the flow of air.

Try this with a harmonica!

- Play the Draw 4 out from the right side of your mouth while you obstruct the holes to the left by putting your tongue in all those holes.

- When you retain Draw 4, whisper "kuh-kuh-kuh" the K-spot is the area at which your tongue meets the top of your mouth.

- Play Draw 4 again. When you sound a note, lift your tongue to concentrate on making a K-spot so that airflow takes place in the reduced passing between your tongue as well as the top of your mouth.

- Ensure you keep on practicing the draw 4 to bend down until you are good at it. So with that stated, this is how you bend a note on the harmonica.

Lesson 8: Blues Harmonica

Ever since the origin of the harmonica, the harmonica has been an essential part of blues music. The blues is a distinctly American form of art that originated from the clash between African and European traditions in the American South. The harmonica also has a natural talent for the blues, with its simplicity in making weeping and shrieking sounds strongly linked with this sort of music.

The Best Harmonica For Playing Blues

Blues is often played on two kinds of harmonicas, diatonic and chromatic. Anyway, the most crucial part about a harmonica is that it's tightly sealed, in tune, and not bound to make you run, turn green, or risk your wellbeing. It also plays comfortably, makes a significant sound, looks pretty good, lasts for years, and doesn't cost a hand or a leg; then it's a star. Your best options are:

Diatonic Harmonica

The diatonic harmonica is the best harmonica for playing blues. When playing blues, you're frequently going to use this harmonica. This harmonica has lots of characteristics which include:

- **Tuning To A Single Key**

    The term diatonic is an artistic slang, which means "mostly in one key." Every diatonic harmonica has notes that pertain to only one key, such as the key of C, G, or B flat. So you're inevitably going to have a few diatonic to play in several keys.

- **Has A Reed For Each Note**

  Diatonic is a solitary reed harmonica, with just one reed for every note. Dual reed harmonicas, such as tremolos, are quite popular, but they're nearly never used in blues.

- **It Has Ten Holes**

  You can also get 4, 6, 10, 12, and 14 holes for diatonic, you can also use all of them to play blues. However, you're going to use the 10-hole diatonic more frequently.

Chromatic Harmonica

I already talked about this harmonica in our previous lesson; however, this sort of harmonica is larger and much more costly than the diatonic, you could use it for one song out of ten. However, its unique tone is an essential factor in the harmony of urban blues.

Blues Harmonica Licks And Riffs

Once you play the blues on your harmonica, you utilize small sequences of notes known as licks and riffs as essential components for lengthier artistic statements. Every riff and lick typically highlights the notes of the chord that are played within the background. Blues musicians frequently highlight the notes of the home chord (the I chord) even if another chord is played. In this way, Blues encourages people to stay close to home.

Riffs sometimes help to clarify the musical style of a song, and you generally repeat it many times in the lyric of a song. Examples involve a distinctive rhythmic bass line that automatically detects a tune until you hear a song or a repetitive melodic line played by song instruments behind an artist.

Licks are generally shorter than riffs, and you can also play them everywhere in a song and mix them with many other licks in various patterns at will. Sometimes a solo guitar player or harmonica player is just a flashy, well-crafted sequence of licks.

Five Riffs Familiar To Most Blues Musician

First Riff

Second Riff

Third Riff

Fourth Riff

Lyrics: I won-der why that dog don't growl

Fifth Riff

Lyrics: I'm a big man. I'm so tall

- The 1st riff is a famous bass line that is frequently played by song instruments. It utilizes the home note as the smallest note (Draw 2) as well as the highest note (Blow 6) and put both the home note over the powerful 1st beat.
- The 2nd riff is a popular flip-era, large-band riff which has also been used with harmonica instrumentals such as Snooky Pryor's "Boogie" and, in a slightly modified edition, Little Walter's "Juke." like in the first riff, it starts and ends on the home note of the song, growing to put the last home note on the very first beat of the bar.
- John Lee Hooker also used the 3rd riff, along with the band Canned Heat, especially on the track "On the Road

Again," showcasing Alan's "Blind Owl" Wilson. Sonny Boy Williamson II also used the same riff for the instrumental support of his track "Help Me."

- The 4th riff is mostly performed by a singer who plays between the riffs. "Hoochie Coochie Man" by Muddy Waters, showcasing Little Walter on harmonica, is possibly the most popular track for using this riff.

- The 5th riff often juxtaposes the claims of the artist. Bo Diddley has used this riff most prominently in "I'm a Guy," featuring Billy Boy Arnold on the harmonica.

How To Play 12-Bar Blues On The Harmonica

Almost all of the blues songs adopt a style known as the 12-bar blues. Besides being twelve-bar in size, the 12 bar blues seems to have its inner workings. Once you understand that logic and then use it to form your words, playing the blues on your harmonica will seem as logical as speaking. The section of 12-bar blues contains three components, and each component is four bars long.

Each of the components does so many things:

- It develops the storyline of the phrases.
- It's develops in the last part.
- It plans the next part.

Most 12-bar blues are only using a single background chord that plays behind the full song. Even so, many other blues songs have a development of the chord or a series of chords. Every part of the blues section begins with a unique chord, which lets you know where you are in the song. The artists have arrived up with millions of variations and complicated explanations on the development of the 12-bar blues chord.

Nevertheless, here I stay with the most simple, down-to-earth edition. It requires only three chords, which could be described by their connections with each other, using Roman numerals:

- The I (one) chord, which is also known as the home chord, is recognized with the key to the song.
- The IV (four) chord, four measures over the I chord.
- The V (five) chord, five measures just above I chord.

The following diagram illustrates 12-bar blues as a chord chart, which reveals the development of the chord as well as how long each chord will last. Every diagonal cut symbolizes one beat, with vertical bar lines signalling the end of each 4-stroke bar. The chords in the parenthesis are voluntary. They don't appear in the most simplified example of the 12-bar blues, but they are used quite often by artists.

How To Play The Harmonica Like A Pro

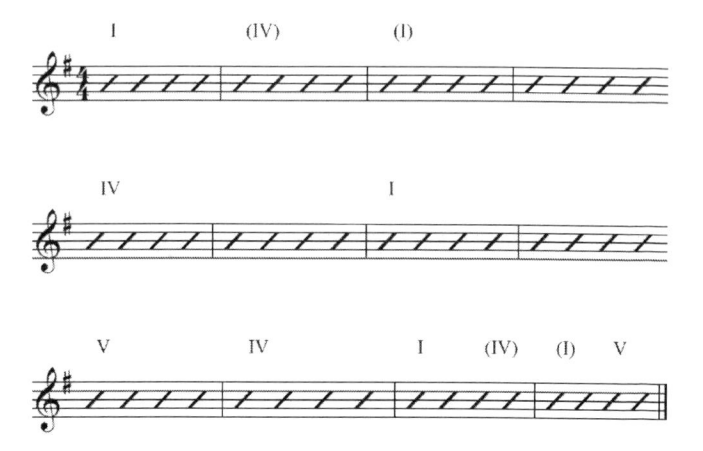

Conclusion

Finally! We've gotten to the conclusion of this book, but before we round it all up,

Guys if you're a fan of chess, or would love to learn how to play the chess, I highly recommend this book.

<u>20 Tactics To Become A Successful Chess Grandmaster</u>

The book is an ultimate turn-based strategic guide that provides you with the fastest, most effective and most enjoyable way to play chess. It helps promote the brain's development at any age, prevent Alzheimer's, and enhance both adults and kids' decision-making skill.

I just published the book and would be given it out for free for 3 days.

So, with that stated, here are the top 5 songs to play on the harmonica.

5 Popular Songs To Play On The Harmonica

Song 16: "Amazing Grace"

Harmonica Type: **Diatonic**

Key: **Any**

3 4 5 4   5   -4   4   4   3
Amazing Grace, how sweet the sound,
3   4   54   5   -456 6
That saved a   wretch like me.
56 65 65   4 5-4 4   4   3
I   once was lost but now am found,
3   4   54   5 -4 4
Was blind, but   now I see.

Higher and snappier 😊

 6 7 8-87   8   -8   7   -6   6
Amazing Grace, how sweet the sound,
6   7   8-87   8   -889 9
That saved a   wretch like me.
89   98   98   7 8-8 7   -6   6
I   once was lost but now am found,
 6-6   7   87   8 -8   7
Was blind, but now I   see.

6 7 8 7   8   -8   7   -6   6
Amazing Grace, how sweet the sound,
6   7 8 7   8 -8 9
That saved a__ wretch like me.
8 9 8 9 8   7   6 -67   7 -6   6
I once was lost but no-w   am__ found,
6   7   8 7   8 -8 7
Was blind, but now I see.

Song 17: "He's Got The Whole World"

Harmonica Type: **Diatonic**

Key: **C**

```
  6    6    5    6     5   4   -6  -6    6
He's  got  the whole wor-ld  in  His hands,

  6    6    5   -5   -4  -3  -6  -6    6
He's  got  the whole wor-ld  in  His hands,

  6    6    5    6     5   4   -6  -6    6
He's  got  the whole wor-ld  in  His hands,

  6    6    5    6     6  -5  -4    4
He's  got  the whole world in  His hands.
```

Song 18: "Roll In My Sweet Baby's Arm"

Harmonica Type: **Diatonic**

Key: **Any**

You can change the note, but this is just how I have always liked it

```
6    6   6   -7     -7  -5    6
Roll in my sweet ba-by's arms.

6    6   6   -7     -7  -8   -6
Roll in my sweet ba-by's arms.

-5   -5  6   6      6   -7
Gon-na lay 'round the shack

-7   -7  7   7      7    5
'til the mail train comes back,

-5   -4   -4  -4 -7    -7 -6   6
And roll in my sweet ba-by's arms.

VERSE 1
-5 6     6   6   -7    -7  -5   6    6
I ain't gon-na work on the rail-road,

-5 6     6   6   -7   -7 -8   -6
I  ain't gon-na work on the farm

-6   -6  6   6      6    -7
Gon-na lay 'round the shack

-7   -7   7   7     7    5
'til the mail train comes back

-5   -4   -4  -4 -7    -7 -6   6
And roll in my sweet ba-by's arms.
```

Song 19: "I Should Have Known Better"

Harmonica Type: **Any**

Key: **Any**

```
6  -6      6   6  5   6  6
I SHOULD HAVE KNO-WN BET-TER

  6  5  6     6  -6
WITH A GIRL LIKE YOU

  6  6  5    6
THAT I WOULD LOVE

 6  5  6    6   6  -6
EV-'RY-THING THAT YOU DO

-6 -6 -6  6  -6  -7  -6 -7  7
AND I DO-HEY,HEY,HEY-AND I DO

-6 -7 -6 -7 -6     -6  -7
WHO-A-WHO-A-CAN'T YOU SEE-

  5      -6 -7  7    -7
THAT'S WHEN I TELL YOU

-6  -5  -6   5
THAT I LOVE YOU

 5  5     -6 -7  7
OH,YOU'RE GON-NA SAY

-7  -6    7  5
YOU LOVE ME TOO

 5   5  -4 5 -4  4
HOO,HOO,HO-O,HO-O,
```

```
5 -4 4  -4   5  6  -5
O-H,AND WHEN I ASK YOU

5  -4  6  6  5  6  8
TO BE MINE----------

-4      5  -5  6
YOU'RE GON-NA SAY

-5   5   -4 -4  4
YOU LOVE ME TOO--
```

Song 20: "When The Levee Breaks"

Harmonica Type: **Diatonic**

Key: **Bb**

```
6 6 6 6 6 6 -6 -6 -6 -6 -6
-6 6 -6 -4
-6 6 -6 -4

-6 -8 -8
6 7 7
-5 -6 -6 7 7 -8

-6 6 -5 -8
-6 6 -5 7
-6 6 -5 7 7 -8
```

111

So, with all that stated, I do hope a lot was learned from this book, and if it seems complicated for you to understand the lessons in this book, be patient, do not rush it, take a break from the book, and come back later to read it. Ensure you follow all the steps listed in this book, and I know you will become a harmonica professional in no time. I wish you the best of luck on your harmonica journey.

Other Books By Same Author

20 Tactics To Become A Successful Chess Grandmaster

About The Author

Tom Wheeler is a harmonica player, musician, writer as well as a teacher based in San Francisco, California. Tom lifelong mission has been to learn the harmonica (and encourage others to do the same) started early on, when he couldn't get a mentor then he had to sort it out the hard way.

As a musician, Tom performs with almost every kind of harmonica in regards to writing, organizing as well as conducting. He is presently performing with the San Francisco Harmonica orchestra, as well as Tin Sandwich.

He persists with enhancing the understanding as well as recognition of the harmonica via internet communities.

NOTES

Printed in Great Britain
by Amazon